Children's Authors

A.A. Milne

Jill C. Wheeler
ABDO Publishing Company

The Man Behind Pooh

In 1996, an English bookstore asked people to list their favorite books from the 1900s. From the answers, the store created a list of the top 100 books in order of popularity. Number 17 on the list was *Winnie-the-Pooh.*

Pooh was created by an Englishman named A.A. Milne. Milne was a well-known magazine writer, novelist, and **playwright**. He wrote mostly for adults. However, he is best remembered for his stories and poems for children.

More than 75 years have passed since Milne introduced the lovable teddy bear who became Winnie-the-Pooh. In that time, Milne's books about Pooh have sold about 70 million copies worldwide. Today, readers still enjoy the adventures of the "Bear of Very Little Brain."

A. A. Milne

Star Student

Alan Alexander Milne was born on January 18, 1882, in London, England. His father, John, ran a small, private boy's school called Henley House. His mother, Sarah Maria, had been a teacher.

Alan was the couple's youngest son. He had two older brothers, Barry and Ken. Alan and Ken were especially close. They loved to ride their bikes and explore the neighborhood.

At age six, Alan began classes at Henley House. He was a star student from the beginning. According to his father, Alan could write more in three minutes than his teacher could read in thirty. This was not surprising, considering Alan had started to read before he was three!

In 1893, Alan began attending Westminster School in London on a **scholarship**. He did well in his classes, especially mathematics. But over time, Alan put less effort into his studies. He wrote poems and stories instead. Some of his writing was published in the *Elizabethan,* the school magazine.

Alan grew up in London, one of the world's oldest and most historic cities.

Becoming a Writer

While at Westminster, Milne read a copy of *Granta*. It was a student magazine published at the University of Cambridge. One of Milne's friends suggested Milne attend school there so he could edit *Granta*. Milne said he would do just that.

Milne completed his studies at Westminster in 1900. He then entered Cambridge's Trinity College on a mathematics **scholarship**. He became the editor of *Granta* two years later. Soon, he was doing more writing than mathematics.

In 1903, Milne graduated from Trinity College with a mathematics degree. Milne's father wanted him to become a teacher or a **civil servant**. But, Milne wanted to be a writer. Specifically, he wanted to write for a popular humor magazine called *Punch*.

With that goal in mind, Milne rented an apartment near the *Punch* offices in London. He wrote stories, essays, and poems. Then he submitted them to magazines and newspapers. Milne hoped they would publish his writing.

Milne's first success was a **parody** of the Sherlock Holmes stories. *Vanity Fair* magazine accepted it. Then in 1904, *Punch* accepted its first piece by Milne. It was a poem called "New Gang." By 1905, *Punch* was regularly publishing Milne's poems and articles.

Trinity College was founded by Henry VIII in 1546.

Dream Job

While writing poetry and articles, Milne also worked on his first book. He published it in 1905. It was called *Lovers in London*. The novel had grown out of a series of stories he had written for the *St. James Gazette*. Meanwhile, Milne was still contributing to *Punch*.

Then in 1906, Milne was offered a new opportunity. That year, a new editor named Owen Seaman began working at *Punch*. He hired Milne as an assistant editor. The position paid little, but Milne didn't mind. He had landed his dream job!

As an assistant editor, Milne had many duties. He edited articles, reviewed books and plays, and contributed his own writing each week. He later published collections of his *Punch* writings in several books.

In December 1910, Seaman invited Milne to a birthday party. It was for Seaman's goddaughter. Her name was Dorothy de Sélincourt. Dorothy's friends called her Daphne. Alan and Daphne enjoyed each other's company from the start. The two married in June 1913.

Punch *magazine stopped publication in 1992. However, it was brought back in 1996 and is still published today.*

Fighting in France

Milne's life unexpectedly changed when **World War I** began in 1914. Thousands of young Englishmen signed up to fight. Milne felt pressure to do the same. He joined the British Army's Royal Warwickshire Regiment in February 1915.

That summer, Milne attended a training course to become a **signaling** officer. After his training, Milne was stationed just off England's southern coast on the Isle of Wight. While there, he wrote plays, including *Once on a Time* and *Wurzel-Flummery*.

In July 1916, Milne was sent to fight in France. But, he grew ill with **trench fever** that November and was sent back to England. Milne spent several weeks in the hospital. Then he returned to the Isle of Wight to train other signaling officers.

Early in 1917, Milne learned that a director was interested in producing *Wurzel-Flummery*. There was only one catch. Milne had to cut the play from three **acts** to two. Milne accepted the challenge, and the play was produced in London that April.

Production of *Wurzel-Flummery* marked the start of the next phase of Milne's writing career. He continued working for the military. Yet, he spent his spare time writing plays. His most famous play was *Mr. Pim Passes By*. Audiences in England and America enjoyed it for years.

A.A. Milne in 1915, around the time he joined the military

A Vacation Project

The Milne family grew in 1920. That year, the Milnes' son, Christopher Robin, was born. They nicknamed him Billy. Just before Billy's first birthday, Daphne visited Harrods department store. She bought a stuffed teddy bear for her son. Before long, Daphne and Billy were making up stories about the bear.

Meanwhile, Milne continued to write plays. He also published another book, *The Red House Mystery*. Then in 1923, Rose Fyleman contacted Milne. She asked him to write a piece for her children's magazine, *Merry-Go-Round*. Milne refused. He told her that he wrote for adults, not children.

Milne soon reconsidered Fyleman's offer. For fun, he wrote a poem called "The Dormouse and the Doctor." Fyleman loved it and printed it in her magazine. She suggested he write more children's verses.

Milne was going to say no. But while on vacation, he grew bored during a rainy spell. Milne decided he would write some poetry. His vacation project turned into an entire book of children's verses.

The book, called *When We Were Very Young*, was published in 1924. Many of the poems were about Billy. Others came from Milne's own childhood memories. The book featured illustrations by E.H. Shepard. It also featured a lovable stuffed bear named Teddy Bear.

The bear Daphne bought for Billy eventually gained fame as Winnie-the-Pooh.

WINNIE THE POOH

15

Winnie-the-Pooh

In 1925, the Milnes bought a country home called Cotchford Farm. It was near woods and streams. Billy loved exploring the countryside. Milne found the setting a great place to create new stories.

Milne's new stories included one old character, Teddy Bear. But, the bear had a new name. It was Winnie-the-Pooh. Winnie was the name of a bear in London Zoo. Pooh was the name Billy had given a swan he'd once seen.

The Winnie-the-Pooh stories included other characters from Billy's stuffed-animal collection. They were a small pig, a donkey, and a kangaroo. Their adventures took place in the Hundred Acre Wood. It looked much like the land around Cotchford Farm.

On December 24, 1925, Winnie-the-Pooh made his **debut**. Milne wrote a story about a bear who uses a balloon to float up to a beehive in a tree. The story ran in London's *Evening News*. It became the first chapter of the book *Winnie-the-Pooh*.

For this book, Milne again worked with illustrator E.H. Shepard. Shepard visited Cotchford Farm. He sketched the farm's land. He also sketched Billy playing with his stuffed animals. These sketches inspired his illustrations in *Winnie-the-Pooh*. The book was published on October 14, 1926.

Billy's stuffed-animal collection included (from left to right) *Kanga, Tigger, Winnie-the-Pooh, Piglet, and Eeyore.*

More Pooh

Winnie-the-Pooh sold well, but not as well as *When We Were Very Young*. So, Milne's publisher requested another book of children's poems. Milne agreed to the assignment and wrote *Now We Are Six*, which was published in 1927. The verses also featured Winnie-the-Pooh.

Milne decided to write one last book about the lovable bear. It was called *The House At Pooh Corner*. It featured a new character named Tigger. The book appeared in October 1928. Milne believed it was his best book.

Soon, life began to change at the Milne household. In 1929, Billy began attending preparatory school at Gibbs'. He was growing up. He

E.H. Shepard illustrated more than 100 books, including Milne's poetry books and Pooh stories.

was less interested in toys and make-believe now. That same year, Milne was saddened by the death of his brother Ken.

At this point in his life, Milne returned to the theater. In 1930, Milne's play *Toad of Toad Hall* was produced. He had written it earlier in his career. It was an adaptation of Kenneth Grahame's *The Wind in the Willows*. *Toad of Toad Hall* is still sometimes performed at Christmastime.

A.A. Milne and Billy spend time together in their home in England.

A Long Career

Milne had been a talented humorist and **playwright** long before his Pooh books. He hoped to regain that reputation after them. However, Milne was never again quite as popular. He disliked being remembered only for his children's books.

Despite his reputation as a children's author, Milne continued to write for adults. In 1934, Milne wrote *Peace with Honour*. In it, Milne discussed why he thought war was a bad way to solve problems. Five years later, Milne also wrote an **autobiography** titled *It's Too Late Now.*

In 1952, Milne suffered a stroke. He underwent a brain operation a few months later. The operation left him

A.A. Milne wrote many plays, poems, articles, and books. However, he is best remembered as the creator of Winnie-the-Pooh.

partially **paralyzed**. He was no longer able to write professionally. His health continued to fail, and he died on January 31, 1956, at Cotchford Farm.

At the time of his death, Milne's children's books had already sold more than 7 million copies. The sales continue to this day. Milne once wrote that he wanted to leave a name that would live forever. With Pooh, he has done just that.

Milne and Daphne in 1950, shortly before he became ill

Glossary

act - one of the main divisions of a play.

autobiography - a story of a person's life that is written by himself or herself.

civil servant - a member of the civil service. The civil service is the part of the government that is responsible for matters not covered by the military, the courts, or the law.

debut - a first appearance.

paralyze - to cause a loss of motion or feeling in a part of the body.

parody - a humorous work in which the author imitates a book, play, story, or song.

playwright - a person who writes plays.

scholarship - a gift of money to help a student pay for schooling.

signaling - a system of flags, morse code, and other signals used by the military to communicate.

trench fever - an illness marked by a high fever and pain in the muscles, bones, and joints.

World War I - from 1914 to 1918, fought in Europe. Great Britain, France, Russia, the United States, and their allies were on one side. Germany, Austria-Hungary, and their allies were on the other side.

Web Sites

To learn more about A.A. Milne, visit ABDO Publishing Company on the World Wide Web at **www.abdopub.com**. Web sites about Milne and Winnie-the-Pooh are featured on our Book Links page. These links are routinely monitored and updated to provide the most current information available.

Today **Winnie-the-Pooh** *is popular all over the world.*

Index